NORTHCOUR

THE STORY OF A HAMLE

by

JUDY THOMAS

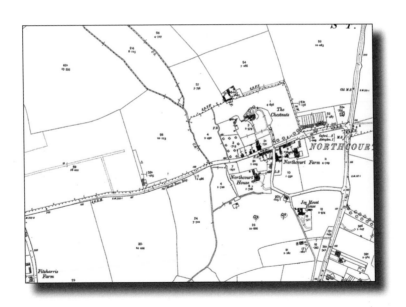

Saint Helen Publishing
33 East Saint Helen Street
Abingdon
Oxfordshire
OX14 5EE

ISBN 978-0-95-604663-5

First published 2022

Design by Ben Jeapes: benjeapes@gmail.com

Cover sky photo by Geri Mis on Unsplash

Cover picture: The sixteenth century barns on Northcourt Road before restoration

ISBN 978-0-95-604663-5

9 780956 046635 >

Introduction

It is difficult for a newcomer to this area to appreciate how small Northcourt was for much of its history. In the 18th and 19th centuries it only had ten or twelve houses, four of which were farms, but for such a small place it has a surprisingly rich history. This book aims to introduce Northcourt to residents, visitors and anyone else who would like to know more about its past.

Acknowledgements

I am most grateful to everyone who has contributed information about Northcourt, especially Margaret Gosling, formerly of Joymount, for the use of material from her unpublished Local History Thesis on Northcourt, and Philip Candy for information and photographs of Northcourt Farm. My thanks to Michael Matthews for filling out my understanding of Abingdon's 1930s expansion, and to Gwyneth Jones for information about her family's wartime experiences in Abingdon. I am grateful to Elizabeth Drury and to my husband Spencer for photographs of Northcourt, to Ben Jeapes for his skill and patience as designer, and to my son Roger Thomas for his invaluable help and advice.

Any errors or omissions are entirely the author's responsibility.

Also by the author

Abingdon in Camera

Abingdon Past & Present

More of Abingdon Past & Present

Pupils and teachers of Northcourt House School with the Head Teacher, Miss Tatham, in 1964.

CONTENTS

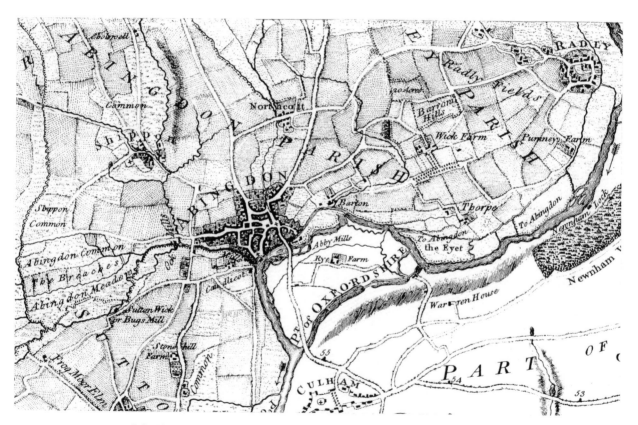

John Rocque's map of Abingdon, 1760. © Oxfordshire History Centre.

1 – The Early History

For much of its existence, Northcourt (variously spelt as Norecott, northcote and Norcot) was a small hamlet situated a mile from the town centre of Abingdon (now in Oxfordshire, but historically in Berkshire). Walk up the Oxford Road past a series of housing estates and turn left into Northcourt Lane. Once known as Dark Lane, it winds between high banks topped with trees and hedges – a reminder of Northcourt's rural origins – until it joins Northcourt Road in the middle of the village.

Little is known about the early history of Northcourt except that Roman coins were found there in the 19th century. Unfortunately the exact findspot was not recorded; however, the area is ideal for settlement, with fertile land watered by the River Stert and two smaller streams. People may have lived here in the Iron Age (pre-Roman) period, when Abingdon itself was a defended settlement or 'oppidum'. Two fields on the east side of the Oxford Road in the Appleford Drive/ Hendred Way area had the names Upper and Lower Wallam. The name derives from the Saxon word 'WEALA' – a Welshman or foreigner – and may refer to a remnant of the Romano-British population still co-existing with early Saxon settlers, as at Barton Court Farm (now part of the Daisy Bank housing estate) where there was a small Roman villa, the site of which was later occupied by early Saxons.

Abingdon Abbey

The most important influence on Northcourt was its relationship to Abingdon's great Benedictine abbey, founded in Saxon times. The abbey owned many manors (or farming estates) locally. Produce and profits from them supported the abbot and the monks, and paid for the abbey's building projects.

Northcourt was a grange, or outlying farm, of the abbey. Northcourt is not mentioned by name in the Domesday Book of 1086 because it formed part of the abbey's huge manor of Barton. This extended from Abingdon to Dry Sandford, Sunningwell and Kennington. The original name was 'north cot' –

a small settlement (or 'cot') north of the town and abbey, so Northcourt was defined by its relationship to Abingdon. Unlike neighbouring villages such as Shippon and Wootton, Northcourt did not have a church. It was probably too small and too close to Abingdon.

Originally, the abbey would have farmed all of the Northcourt land. The monks were expected to do manual work, and they could have walked the mile or so from the abbey to Northcourt each day

The thirteenth century tithe barn.

to oversee or to help with the work there. They may have used a building on Northcourt Lane where the Old Farmhouse is now during the day, but returned to the abbey to sleep.

In 1184-85, the Abbey Chronicle mentions Northcourt as being assigned to the 'Monk of the Works' – monachus de opere – who was responsible for the abbey buildings, because the income from farming Northcourt was dedicated

to the upkeep of the fabric of the great abbey church of St. Mary and the buildings round the cloister, all of which were destroyed when King Henry VIII ordered the dissolution of the monasteries. (The ruins in the Abbey Grounds are a Victorian folly.) Produce such as grain and wool would have been stored in the splendid 13th century stone barn (often called the tithe barn) which still survives today.

2 – The Medieval Period

The Abingdon Abbey Cartularies or Charters, a collection of legal documents which cover the 12th to the 14th centuries, give an interesting picture of life in Northcourt at this period. There seems to have been a thriving community, necessary for the cultivation of such a large area of land. Plough-land was farmed in strips, with teams of oxen used for ploughing. Some strips appear to have been privately owned, others belonged to Abingdon Abbey, and the abbey was frequently involved in litigation to recover land in private hands which they claimed to be theirs.

In the 12th and 13th centuries, Northcourt would have looked very different from the small hamlet which it later became. Many individuals would have worked plots or strips of land in Northcourt Field, which at that time probably comprised much of what we think of as North Abingdon today (see page 4).

For over 200 years after the Norman Conquest in 1066, England enjoyed a time of settled weather and growth. But after years of relative prosperity, a change in the climate in the 14th century brought colder, wetter weather; the abbey eventually had to abandon its vineyard (which was situated near today's road called the Vineyard); there were diseases of sheep and cattle; harvests failed and people were starving. There was also political unrest which particularly targeted the wealthy abbeys such as Abingdon and Bury St Edmund's.

Northcourt was not immune from such troubles, which beset the abbey from time to time. The townspeople of Abingdon resented the abbey's dominance over their affairs, and especially its tight control over the town's markets. These tensions led to serious riots against the abbey in 1327. The townspeople first stopped traders from coming to the market, and then prevented the abbot's bailiffs from collecting fees and other profits, attacking and beating them 'to the abbey's loss and detriment'. They then attacked the abbey at night, burning the recently-built guildhall (on the site of the present County Hall) on the way, but they were repulsed at the abbey gateway with two townsmen killed. A few nights later, having recruited the help of the Commonalty or Corporation of Oxford, who had no love for the clerks and clerics of the university and were equally happy to have a go at the monks of Abingdon, the rabble came from Oxford, burning abbey properties in Northcourt and Barton before breaking into the abbey precinct.

Northcourt got off lightly compared to the abbey itself where buildings were damaged, chests broken open and documents burned; some monks were attacked and goods valued at £20,000 were carried off by the rioters. The abbot and some of the senior monks escaped by boat across the river and only returned several months later with an armed guard.

The goods and chattels taken from the abbot's house and church were valued at £10,000; vestments and gold and silver cups, linen and woollen cloth and 1,000 carcases of sheep, 100 of oxen and 300 sides of bacon were valued at a further £1,000. This story may have grown in the telling; did the abbey really have space to store such a huge quantity of meat? And had the monks abandoned the strict Benedictine rule which, at least in the early years of the abbey, forbade the consumption of meat from four-footed animals such as cows, sheep, goats and rabbits? And how did the fifty or so named rioters manage to carry away so much stuff? Although much of the stolen property was reclaimed, it took many years for the abbey to recover.

In 1348 the bubonic plague known as the Black Death swept through England, carrying off a third to a half of the population. Abbot Roger's death in 1361 was attributed to the plague, and the abbey had to ordain many new young priests to replace those who had died. Priests would have been particularly at risk because of their duty to attend the sick and dying. Few local records of the Black Death survive, but Northcourt must have been affected like everywhere else. It was generally reckoned that it took 200 years for the country to recover, and further outbreaks of plague occurred in subsequent centuries.

However, everyday life must have carried on and people continued to go about their business. Thus in 1375/76 we find the aptly-named William Scissor de Northcot (a tailor) mentioned in the Abbey Treasurer's accounts – one of the few ordinary people of medieval Northcourt whose name has survived over the generations.

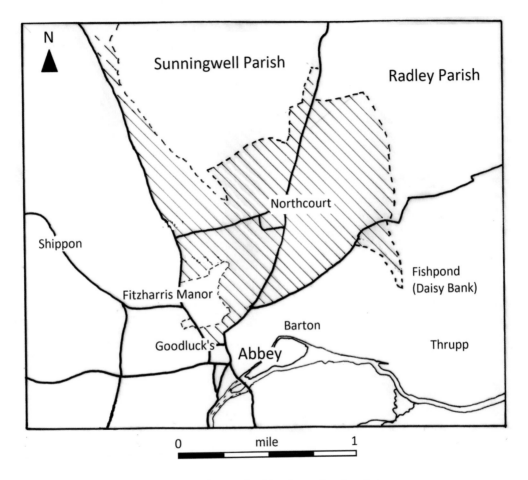

N

Sunningwell Parish

Radley Parish

Northcourt

Shippon

Fitzharris Manor

Fishpond
(Daisy Bank)

Goodluck's

Barton

Thrupp

Abbey

0   mile   1

The Northcourt land in the medieval period.

So, how large was the abbey's Northcourt estate? It is hard to be sure, but it may have covered around 450 acres. It seems to have extended to the parish boundaries of Sunningwell to the north and Radley to the east, and to the Radley Road and Wootton Road on the south and west. At the time of the Norman Conquest, some of this area was separated off to create Fitzharry's Manor for FitzHenry, a Norman knight, but the abbey later recovered most of this land. As time went on, the abbey leased out more land instead of farming it directly. This included Lynge's Farm or Goodluck's Farm, discussed below. The two Abingdon Cartularies mentioned above also contain references to disputes over the ownership of other strips of farmland in 'Northcourt Field'. One of these properties included a house in Northcourt and some pasture. Pasture and meadow were very important, because grass and hay were needed to feed the oxen and other animals, especially over the winter.

An area called Daisy Bank (now the Abbey Fishponds Nature Reserve) was also part of Northcourt, providing valuable pasture in a largely arable area. Here, an earth dam was built across a stream valley to create a fishpond, perhaps to provide fish for the monks. The road from Abingdon to Radley crossed the dam in the medieval period, and the line is still a public footpath today. The route of today's Radley Road would probably have been under water, or at least very boggy, when the fishpond dam was in use, because of the two streams which cross the road at this point. The valley also contained peat which could be dug up and used as fuel.

Northcourt is mentioned again in 1372 in a legal agreement over where the abbey's tenants and servants should worship and which of Abingdon's two medieval churches, St Nicolas or St Helen's, should receive their tithes and parochial dues. Under the agreement, Abingdon became a divided parish; it remained so until 1894 when St Nicolas and St Helen's were amalgamated to become a single parish.

St Nicolas was granted the abbey site, together with several detached areas – Northcourt, Fitzharris and Ock Mill. These were abbey properties where servants of the abbey lived or worked. At Northcourt this included land around the farmhouse and farm buildings, with an adjacent close or field, and a separate portion of arable and pasture connected by a long narrow roadway, possibly the monks' path to their properties at Sunningwell

– hence its modern name of Monks' Way. The parish boundary runs through the Old Farmhouse along the passage from the front to the back door. In the annual 'beating of the bounds' ceremony (a procession around the parish boundary), a cross would be cut in the lintel over the back door to remind people where the boundary ran. St Nicolas parish was described as the area on which people connected with the abbey 'actually or constructively dwelt', so it's odd that the tithe barn and most of the Old Farmhouse were not included in St Nicolas parish. One possible explanation is that the present large lounge to the right of the front door, with its huge fireplace, may originally have been a kitchen separate from the main house to reduce the risk of fire, where the farm workers took their meals. A rickety old

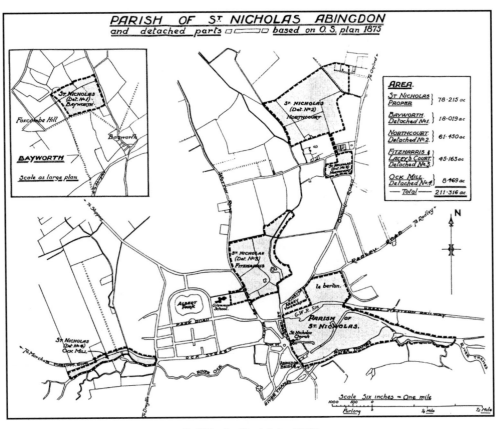

St Nicolas Parish in 1372.

wooden staircase in one corner gave access to a large upstairs room where the resident workers could also have slept.

'Beating the Bounds' was an ancient custom designed to remind local inhabitants of the boundaries of their land, at a time when there were few maps and most ordinary people were illiterate. Groups of people, including young boys, would walk round the borough boundary with the mayor and town councillors, or with the vicar and churchwardens for the ecclesiastical boundary. They would make a cross on significant rocks or trees, stopping occasionally to sing a hymn or to take lunch (asparagus was popular!) as the process took two days. If the boundary ran through the middle of a river then the officials could get into a boat, or the boys would swim. They were sometimes beaten to help them to remember. The custom of 'Beating the Bounds' lapsed with the development of maps and universal education, and ended in the mid 19th century.

After the Black Death in 1348, the abbey increasingly leased out its land to tenants because of the shortage of labour. However, in 1473-4 when Florence Wolley was Monk of the Works, the abbey was still working land at Northcourt itself.

One of the last acts of the abbey before the Dissolution was to lease Lynge's (or Goodluck's) farm to John Kepe in October 1537. This had 92 acres of land, and the buildings were behind Broad Street and Bath Street. Like many former abbey properties, it was granted to the newly-formed Borough of Abingdon in its Charter of 1556, but over fifty years later, James I's Charter of 1609 still mentions a Monk of the Works as 'lately' owning 92 acres in Abingdon fields, part of the manor of Norecotte!

3 – After the Dissolution

Abingdon Abbey was one of the first large abbeys to be dissolved in 1538. The abbot and senior monks were compliant with the king's orders and signed away their rights, unlike the abbot of Reading Abbey who refused to sign and was hung, drawn and quartered for his pains.

It is said that Henry VIII planned to use Abingdon Abbey as a royal hunting lodge, but his assessors told him that the buildings were in too bad a condition, so they were demolished and the stone and lead were taken by barge to London for the king's building projects, such as Hampton Court.

After the dissolution of the abbey, the history of Northcourt was closely connected to the Manor of Radley. In 1569, this manor was bought by George Stonhouse, who already had tenants in Northcourt and Thrupp (a small and ancient settlement near the Thames, today close to the Barton Lane Science Park, off Audlett Drive). The St Nicolas portion of Northcourt was bought from the Crown in 1547 by John Lyon, a large-scale speculator in abbey lands. One of Lyon's descendants married Humfrey Hyde, four times Mayor of Abingdon between 1579 and 1601, and the land at Northcourt passed through a succession of Humfrey Hydes. In a valuation of 1678 the Old Farmhouse is described as 'the Parsonage' – perhaps because of its association with the abbey, as there is no record of a priest having lived there, and Northcourt never had a church.

There is no mention of Northcourt during the English Civil War of the 1640s but it must have been in a difficult situation. Abingdon was occupied twice – first by Royalist troops who were holding the town as part of a protective shield for King Charles I's headquarters at Oxford, and later by a Parliamentary garrison under General Brown after the Royalist garrison unexpectedly pulled out of Abingdon and decamped to Oxford. For the rest of the war, Abingdon was occupied by Parliamentary troops and was a threat to the Royalists who made frequent attempts to retake the town. Sickness was rife and there was little food within a ten-mile radius, so small bands of troops had to run the gauntlet of royalist patrols to find food, and it is recorded that 'they plundered the countrymen's houses of bread, beer and bacon in spite of the pitiful complaints of the poor people.' No doubt Northcourt must have been one of the first places to suffer, given its proximity to Abingdon.

A completely unknown cemetery of Civil War date was discovered during excavations on the abbey site in 1989, including a mass burial of seven soldiers. Research into St Helen's burial records for the period showed that these were Irish mercenaries drafted into the Royalist army, who had been captured and imprisoned in the town gaol. Parliament had decreed that such Irish soldiers should be summarily shot, giving rise to Abingdon's unsavoury reputation as 'the town where execution precedeth triall'.

The Civil War was a troubled time for the whole area, but peace and relative stability returned after the restoration of the monarchy in 1660.

In 1707 the Northcourt estate was sold to Sir John Stonhouse of Radley, who built a handsome new residence, Radley Hall, in 1724. Maybe the profits from Northcourt helped to pay for this.

In 1733, Sir John's daughter Anne married Sir William Bowyer, Baronet, of Denham Court, in Buckinghamshire. Anne and William's grandson died in 1792 without a male heir, so the estate passed to a nephew, Sir George Bowyer. He moved to Radley Hall in 1794. He had lost a leg earlier that year at the naval battle of Ushant, and was made vice-admiral and given the baronetcies of Radley and Denham for his bravery.

Sir George Bowyer died in 1799 and was succeeded by his son, the second Sir George Bowyer. He, however, got into severe financial difficulties, partly as a result of speculating for coal on his land at Bayworth. He had even dug part of a canal to transport it to the Thames – an expensive fiasco. In 1815 the contents of Radley Hall were sold by auction, including 'truly valuable furniture, 1600 volumes of books, valuable paintings and 336 dozen choice wines'. Sir George Bowyer then took his family to live in Italy until his death in 1860, although his son, the third Sir George Bowyer, later returned to the area. From 1819 to 1844, Radley Hall and 112 acres of parkland were leased to Benjamin Kent for a Nonconformist School. In 1847 it was leased again, this time as an Anglican boarding school for boys, which is now

Radley Hall in the 1830s, drawn by Eliza Kent. Reproduced by kind permission of Radley College.

the prestigious Radley College.

Other portions of the original Northcourt Manor went elsewhere, and were combined in the 18th century to form the estate purchased in 1802 by Henry Knapp, the head of a firm of Abingdon bankers – Knapp, Tomkins & Goodall. In 1805, Knapp demolished the old farmhouse on the site and built a fine mansion known as Northcourt House, although he kept the old farm buildings.

His son, also Henry Knapp, inherited the estate on his father's death in 1825, living the life of a prosperous country gentleman and businessman, running his bank and his farm, whose buildings lay just behind the house. Unfortunately he went bankrupt in 1847. There were many private banks in the 19th century, but they were always prone to failure – in 1825, seventy banks had failed in a period of six weeks. Another financial crisis in 1847 resulted in the failure of many more, including Knapp & Co.

Knapp's bankruptcy must have had a considerable impact on Northcourt, three of whose residents – James Williams, William Pitt and Elizabeth Leader – had deposits in his bank, ranging from £85 to £150, but this was small

Northcourt House.

compared to the impact on Knapp himself who had lost his livelihood, home and good name. In November 1847 his farming stock was sold at auction, followed in early December by a three-day sale of his household effects, including furniture, china, glass, linen, carriages, wine and a greenhouse including two prized orange trees. Finally, in January 1848 the house, farm buildings, gardens, cottages and 162 acres were sold. Knapp lost his office of Alderman and in 1850 he was removed as a Governor of Christ's Hospital. There is no further mention of him in local records.

The biggest impact locally was that the bulk of

Henry Knapp's estate, which he had mortgaged for £8,000 just two years earlier, was sold to the third Sir George Bowyer. This purchase included Northcourt House. Bowyer then bought Joymount with 8 acres of land, and Barton Farm in 1849, by which time he owned nearly the whole of Northcourt except for a few small holdings, notably that of James Williams, a local farmer.

In 1883 the third Sir George Bowyer died at the age of 71. His many local charitable works, discussed later (p.28), had made great demands on his resources. He had taken out three mortgages on Northcourt House, two of which were held by the trustees of a marriage settlement on Lady Jane Swinburne, the mother of the poet, Algernon Swinburne. This explains the name of Swinburne Road.

On 15th December 1886 the valuable collection of paintings in Northcourt House was sold at auction. It included works by Turner, Lely, Poussin, Sir George Kneller, Correggio, Zucchero, Canaletto and two Rembrandts. Radley Hall, the park and farms – in all about 1,277 acres – were being leased to Radley College. But it was not enough to keep the creditors at bay. A few days later the third mortgagee, Mr Hoare, foreclosed on the Bowyer estate. The following year, 1887, the Swinburne Trustees foreclosed on Mr Hoare and Northcourt House became the property of the Swinburne Trust, and in 1889 the whole Bowyer estate was put up for sale.

Over the years the Swinburne Trust acquired many more Northcourt properties such as Northcourt Farm, The Chestnuts, and land on both sides of the Oxford Road, including that on which Our Lady's Abingdon School (formerly the Convent) now stands. The Tatham family became tenants of Northcourt House and in 1902 they purchased the property. Part of the purchase price went to pay off the outstanding mortgage and the rest to the Swinburne Trust, and the Tathams bought other properties from the Trust in 1905 and 1916.

The Northcourt Farm buildings at the time of the 1902 sale were typical of a mixed farm of the period and were still dominated by horses. They consisted of a carriage house, harness room, two fowl houses, three spacious barns, a cart stable for six horses, a nag stable for two horses, a cow shed for eight cows, two piggeries, a lean-to shed for five cows, three enclosed yards and cattle sheds and a spanned roof cart shed. There is no mention of the old bothy because this was an integral part of the two piggeries (see illustration on page 14).

It would have housed the pigs underneath with the swineherd or farmhand sleeping above. Although the bothy looks like a cottage, the ceiling was only four feet high, so he would have taken his meals in the big farmhouse kitchen (the present lounge) with the other farmhands.

The Northcourt Farm bothy.

4 – Farming in Northcourt

The Northcourt land used to be farmed with a mixture of arable, some pasture and gardens.

The soil is light and gravelly on the whole so, as was common by this time, a four field rotation

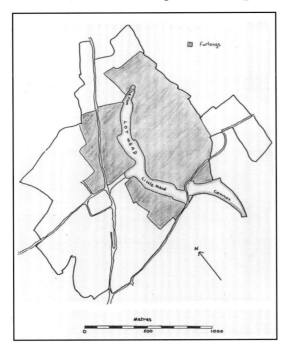

Northcourt Field in 1835 before enclosure, by Margaret Gosling.

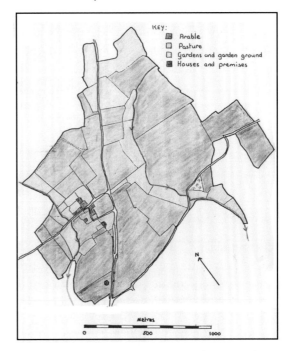

Map of land use in 1842, by Margaret Gosling.

was used with wheat, vetches, peas and turnips, followed by barley, followed by oats, then wheat again, or wheat, peas, beans or turnips, followed by barley and some vetches, followed by fallow, then wheat again. Many of these crops may have been used for animal fodder – in 1847, at the time of his bankruptcy, Henry Knapp had 33 pigs and 169 sheep. Sheep were used to tread the light ground before wheat was planted, and the animals provided manure as well as wool, meat and bacon. There were not many cows because Northcourt had only 32 acres of pasture, whereas William Stacey who farmed the meadows round Barton near the River Thames had 121 acres of pasture.

The 1835 map on page 15 shows Lot Mead, an area of pasture alongside the stream and the common land at Daisy Bank (once the abbey's fishpond). The name Lot Mead refers to the practice of drawing lots to allocate the hay harvest on strips of common land such as these meadows. Small wooden balls with the strip numbers, and others with the villagers' names, were drawn out of two leather bags by a lady such as the lady of the manor. The new owner's initials were cut into the turf at the top of each strip. After the hay harvest the villagers were free to graze their animals all over the meadows. This was considered a fair way of allocating the land when some strips were more productive than others.

The Inhabitants

Most of Northcourt's residents would originally have been involved in farming, but over the centuries the status of the inhabitants gradually changed. In 1547 after the dissolution of the abbey there were ten resident occupiers in Northcourt. Most were small farmers and peasant landholders, with just one gentleman who had the largest holding of 100 acres. By 1678 the number of small farmers had increased from four to six, but the cottagers holding less than a yardland (30 acres) had gone down from six to two. By 1842 (after the enclosure of the open field with its individual strips) the small farmers had also disappeared and most of the land was in the hands of a few large farmers. The only small farmer was Henry Knapp, and he was a gentleman for whom farming was a secondary interest to running his bank.

In many English villages you find several generations of the same families farming the same land, but not in Northcourt. This was probably because of its proximity to Abingdon, where land tended to be bought up by local businessmen as an investment and

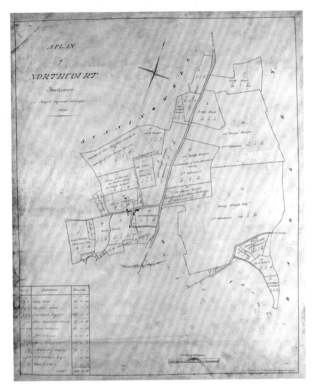

Northcourt Enclosure Map, 1841.
© Berkshire Record Office.

Number	Reference	Quantity
		a. r. p.
1 & 2	Lady Read	32 . 0 . 34
3	Sir John Read	12 . 1 . 2
5.6.7.8.9. 25.26.28. 30.36.37	Sir George Bowyer	160 . 0 . 8
10	John Fountaine's Charity	27 . 0 . 30
11.12.13.16	James Williams	35 . 0 . 35
15	Mr Sellwood	2 . 0 . 3
19.20.21. 23.24.31. 32.34.35.	Henry Knapp Esqr	152 . 3 . 2
27	Morland & Godfrey	8 . 0 . 7
17 & 18	T.H. Graham Esqre	1 . 0 . 22
33	Gravel Pit	. 2 . 12
	Total	431 . 1 . 35

Northcourt Enclosure Map, 1841 – schedule of landowners.
© Berkshire Record Office.

leased out to tenants. Some small landholders probably disappeared in the early 18th century, possibly when the manor was sold to the Stonhouses in 1707.

In 1710 a businessman called John Fountain, who was a prominent Baptist, began buying up Northcourt property. This started a strong Baptist connection with Northcourt which lasted till 1871 as he gradually leased properties to other Baptists. William Rawlins of Northcourt built two small cottages on the north side of Northcourt Road. On his death in 1793, all Rawlins' property passed into the hands of Baptists. The four labourers' cottages on the south side of Northcourt Road (also Rawlins' property) were bought by Bridget Petty and Edward Leader, an executor of Rawlins' will. By 1798 the rest of Rawlins' property was also owned by Edward Leader. He and his wife Elizabeth retired to one of their Northcourt properties in 1822. Her husband died in 1833 but another Baptist, James Williams, helped Elizabeth to remain in the house, where she continued to entertain visiting ministers in spite of total blindness. She died in 1870, shortly before her 102nd birthday; the following year James Williams left the village, thus ending the long association of Baptists with Northcourt.

By 1842 the only old house that was still the home of a man farming Northcourt land was the 'Parsonage', now called the 'Old Farmhouse'. In the course of the 19th century, there was a big increase in the population but no new houses had been built, so three of the four cottages on the south side of Northcourt Road were each divided into two, to provide homes for the cottagers who by then were landless labourers. Thus four houses became seven.

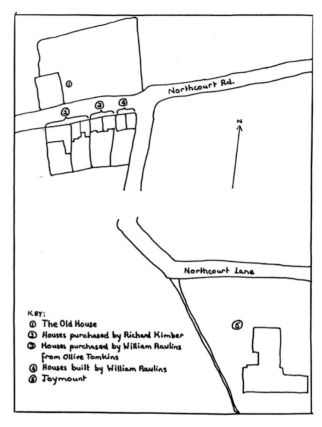

The divided cottages on the south side of Northcourt Road, by Margaret Gosling.

5 – Northcourt Houses

If we look at Northcourt in the later 19th century we can see that it had changed little over the years and there were still only sixteen houses.

The Chestnuts (Terrington House).

The Chestnuts, or Terrington House, was a handsome villa of the late 18th century, built some time before 1797 and demolished in about 1963 to

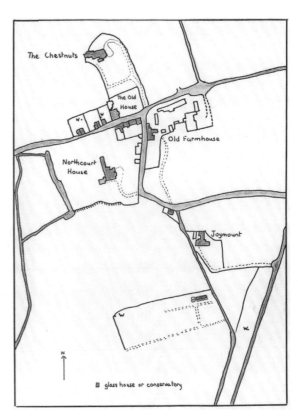

Northcourt houses in the 19th century, by Margaret Gosling.

build Shelley Close, Terrington Close and part of the Sellwood Road/South Avenue development. Its last owners were the Frearsons, a local farming family.

Many villages have an 'Old House' – usually the oldest house in the village, as the name implies. Northcourt has two – the Old House and the Old Farmhouse, both of which were said to be abbey properties, which suggests that they were in existence at the dissolution of the abbey.

The Old House is built of stone with very thick walls. The street front shows that it was originally a three-storey building which was later enlarged and the roof raised. The original house had two

The south front of the Old House showing different phases of building.

The east front of the Old House (from the garden), with a later addition to the north.

good square rooms, with a through passage of well-worn stone flags and a staircase leading to the upper floors. Local tradition says that this was where meals were prepared for the abbey's workers, and the large fireplace occupying the whole of the west wall in the front room supports this. This former farmhouse later became a dairy run from a lean-to extension on the west side of the building.

The east or garden side was refronted and the windows still have the original window catches of c.1650, according to architectural historian Malcolm Airs, so the house itself could be at least 200 years older. Unfortunately, when the roof was replaced some years ago no record was made of the old roof construction, so this useful dating evidence has been lost.

Again according to local tradition, the Old Farmhouse on Northcourt Lane was abbey property, used by the monks when they came up from the abbey to work on the farm. It has seen many changes over the years, but may originally have been a hall house with a single long room with a raised area at one end, later divided into two with what is now a small study with a large fireplace, probably of 16th century date, at one end. The very large sitting room to the right of the front

The Old Farmhouse on Northcourt Lane.

door has a huge fireplace, and may originally have been a kitchen detached from the main house where the farm workers could have had their meals. It once had a rickety old wooden staircase to an upper room, possibly sleeping quarters for the resident farm workers.

Six small cottages were built on the north side of Northcourt Road between 1841 and 1861. The old cottages on the south side of the road may have been built in the 17th century; they were often used to house the employees of Northcourt House.

Mr and Mrs John Loader outside no. 16 (now 22) Northcourt Road, in about 1890.

Cottages on the north side of Northcourt Road.

Joy Loader (later Mrs Marriott) outside 16 Northcourt Road in about 1930.

The Loaders brought up nine children in this cottage which their family occupied for at least three generations, so two houses were knocked into one to accommodate them. John (1845-1919) and one of his sons were gardeners to the Tatham family of Northcourt House. The Loader's granddaughters, Joy and Irma, later married the twin Marriott brothers. Ken Marriott was a caretaker at Dunmore Primary School.

The last house in the row became a pub, first mentioned in 1860 as The Eagle. During World War 1, the name and the pub sign were changed

An outing of regulars from the Spread Eagle pub, with the landlord, Mr Mattingley (centre) with glasses and hat. Mr Mattingley ran the pub from the early 1930s until 1959.

*Cottages on Northcourt Road and
the Spread Eagle pub today.*

Northcourt House.

to the Spread Eagle because of its resemblance to the German eagle.

Northcourt House, the finest house in the village, is a handsome early 19th century mansion, said to be a perfect cube, with a substantial extension to the rear. It was sometimes rented out or remained empty; it has been used as a small private school and for offices; and it also provided extra accommodation for the College of Education further along Northcourt Road. Some of the

The thatched gardener's cottage on Northcourt Lane, painted by Betty Ansell, reproduced by permission of Mrs Mellor.

ancillary buildings have been converted for housing in recent years, and two bungalows have been built in the grounds behind the high stone wall along Northcourt Road.

At some time between 1851 and 1861, a small cottage was built in Northcourt Lane near the entrance to Northcourt House for the coachman, and later the gardener. It was brick with a thatched roof – probably the last thatched cottage in Abingdon. It was pulled down before the houses in Lyon Close were built in the 1990s. More recently another substantial cottage, Wall Cottage, was built in Northcourt Lane just inside the garden wall of Northcourt House, and a former owner of the Old Farmhouse built a large cottage at the end of her garden.

Further down Northcourt Lane is Joymount, another large farmhouse built mainly in the 17th century with later additions, although one wing

Joymount.

was subsequently demolished. When Joymount was for sale in 1905 it came with 75 acres of land, described as '57 unique building sites', located mainly between the Oxford and Radley Roads and Norman Avenue. Joymount originally had a long drive from the Oxford Road before the land was sold for development, but now the main access is to the back of the building from Northcourt Lane.

The Boundary House was built by the Viney family as their home in 1922 (they owned a large furniture shop in West St Helen Street). The name commemorates the extension of the Borough boundary to Northcourt in 1892. The house was leased to Cecil Kimber, the Managing Director of the MG Car Company, from 1933 to 1938. Mr Viney was called up and evacuees lived there during part of the Second World War. Mrs Viney went back to live over the shop in West St Helen Street, but the family returned to the Boundary House after the war.

In 1960 it was converted to a pub, to the dismay of the parishioners of nearby All Saints Methodist Church, but their fears of disturbance happily turned out to be unfounded.

Richard and Marie Viney in front of their home, the Boundary House, in about 1948.

6 – Nineteenth Century Changes

Abingdon was already beginning to expand in the 19th century with the building of the Workhouse in 1835, and four houses on the east side of the Oxford Road north of the Vineyard. The estate of the bankrupt Henry Knapp was bought by another (the third) Sir George Bowyer in 1848. He bought other land nearby in the following years, and by 1850 owned nearly all of Northcourt. In that year, he became a Catholic through the Oxford Movement, with far-reaching consequences for the whole Northcourt area.

In 1854 a Catholic Mission was established in Abingdon. Sir George donated four acres of land at the junction of the Oxford and Radley Roads, and paid for a Church and Presbytery to be built there. Then in 1860, Mother Clare Moore of the Irish Sisters of Mercy, who had been in the Crimea with Florence Nightingale, arrived in Abingdon with some of her nuns to open a school. The nuns were initially housed in part of Joymount and soon began teaching with just one pupil. In 1862 they moved to one of the semi-detached houses

The part of Joymount which was occupied by the nuns.

The Catholic Church of Our Lady & St Edmund of Abingdon.

on the Oxford Road near the newly-built Catholic Church. By 1871 their numbers had increased to seven nuns and seventeen pupils. Mother Clare would surely have met and reminisced with Charlotte Cox, an Abingdon resident who had also been a nurse in the Crimea.

Meanwhile, the population of Northcourt was changing; by 1861 no fewer than six houses were occupied by Catholics, which must have been quite a shock for the resident Baptists, such as Mrs Leader who we are told had an intense 'fear and dread of Popery'. Northcourt House was occupied by George Eyston and his family (presumably a relative of the Catholic Eystons from East Hendred) and there were several Irish households. With a big increase in population but no new houses, over-crowding was rife. The opening of the Eagle pub in 1860 must have provided a welcome escape.

The tithe barn, when it was still part of a working farm.

By 1871 Northcourt House, The Chestnuts and the Old House were no longer working farms, and only Northcourt Farm was still involved in agriculture.

With its medieval stone barn and large farmyard, this was always the most important of the Northcourt farms. It is interesting that this abbey farm should have survived right up to 1945. It then continued as a dairy until 1996; now the whole site apart from the Old Farmhouse belongs to Christ Church.

We get an accurate picture of Northcourt residents for the first time with the 1881 Census. There were 18 households with a total of 41 adults and 53 children. There was one farmer and a shepherd, and most of the men were still working as agricultural labourers or gardeners, apart from a coachman and a carman (cart driver), while the women were either domestic servants or needlewomen. Some of the latter may have worked at Clarke's clothing factory in West St Helen Street making working men's corduroy trousers, but many local women worked for Clarke's doing 'piecework' from home, sewing buttons and buttonholes on the made-up garments.

Following the death of the third Sir George Bowyer in 1883, the Bowyer estate was sold off (see page 13) and many of its Northcourt properties were

Northcourt farmyard in the snow. The bothy is on the left with the Old Farmhouse (centre) and cowshed, (right).

acquired by the Swinburne Trust. The Tatham family became tenants of Northcourt House and purchased the property in 1902. They also bought Northcourt Farm at around the same time.

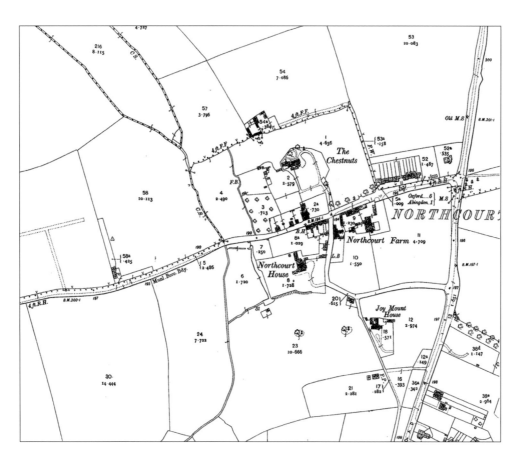

Ordnance Survey map of 1912. Northcourt Terrace was built in around 1910.

7 – Into the Twentieth Century

Expansion into the countryside north of Abingdon started in the late 1800s with half a dozen houses beside a field path (now North Avenue). Known as New Northcourt, there were no other houses until you came to Northcourt Road with its terrace of houses and Northcourt Lodge on the corner with Oxford Road. These had all been built in the early 20th century, some time before 1910, and at a stroke they almost doubled the size of Northcourt. It was a taste of things to come.

Northcourt Terrace today.

Some Northcourt Residents

The Tathams of Northcourt House played an important part in Northcourt in the first half of the 20th century. Mr Tatham was a university professor who ran a 'crammer' in the house, coaching boys for exams and university entrance. He was highly thought of. An obituary in *The Times* in 1945 for a member of the Barings banking family stated: 'He was educated at Eton, *Abingdon with the best of tutors, Meaburn Tatham*, and Cambridge' (author's emphasis). The Tathams had three daughters; the youngest, Evelyn, later ran a preparatory school in the house, and the family were generous benefactors to the community, donating land for the Tatham Hall, the predecessor of today's Northcourt Centre. They leased land to the football and cricket clubs, and placed restrictive covenants on the Northcourt Farm site and the field behind Northcourt House to protect them from future development.

One of the best-known residents of Northcourt at this period was the artist William Blandford Fletcher, a member of the Newlyn School of painters.

He lived in Northcourt Lodge on the corner of Northcourt Road and Oxford Road from about 1915 until his death in 1936, and painted several views of Abingdon, this one of the Tithe Barn being one of the finest.

Northcourt Lodge.

Photograph of the artist William Blandford Fletcher (1858-1936). Reproduced by permission.

The Newlyn School in 1885 with Blandford Fletcher (centre) in light clothes. Reproduced by permission.

Painting of the Tithe Barn by Blandford Fletcher, © Philip Candy.

He was something of a recluse in later life, and was often to be seen walking around Northcourt dressed in an Inverness cape and tweed deerstalker cap. His wife, Mrs Fletcher, rode a tricycle and was the first president of Northcourt Women's Institute.

Another artistic resident of Northcourt at this time was Betty Ansell. A friend, Mrs Fairthorne,

Drawing of Northcourt Farm, by Betty Ansell.

invited Betty and her mother to live in the Old Farmhouse in the 1930s; Betty's attic bedroom overlooked the farmyard and she painted several views of the farm with a cow grazing in the field.

Possibly the best-known Northcourt artist in the post-war period was Ken Messer, who lived in South Avenue for many years. His landscapes and townscapes are still highly sought-after.

8 – Peace and War

The inter-war period was a time of expansion into the countryside around Abingdon.

The Boundary House (now a pub)

The Boundary House (see above) had been built in 1922. At around this time, bungalows and houses started to be built on both sides of the Oxford Road and along Northcourt Road.

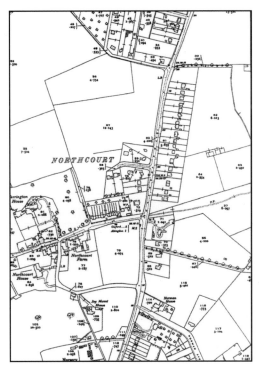

Ordnance Survey map of 1937, showing new housing along Oxford Road.

In 1935 the Workhouse opposite the Catholic Church was demolished to create the Abbott Road and Thesiger Road estate, and Northcourt saw new housing on Sellwood Road and both sides of the Oxford Road. Many business people such as the Coxeters, Brewers and Harris & Matthews, the seed and corn merchants in the Old Gaol, who had lived 'over the shop' – some without bathrooms or gardens – were typical of the families who moved out of the town centre. Mr Harris had started renting Joymount in 1905 and it was bought by his son in 1952. The Matthews family moved into 65 Oxford Road (then 'Windrush') in 1936. Behind the house there was still farm land belonging to Oxford Road Farm owned by Mr Cottrell, an Abingdon butcher, where cows and horses grazed. Only a wire fence separated the gardens from the fields, which were good for mushrooming. The lane to the farm buildings was on the line of the present footpath, from which you could walk across the fields to the Radley Road and Daisy Bank, a popular local picnic spot. On the field side of the hedge lining the farm track were a number of old fruit trees – Victoria plums, greengages and Blenheim apples, which came in useful later in the war years.

In 1937, James (Jim) Candy, who was farming at Milton Hill, heard that the lease of Northcourt Farm was available. The farm buildings were situated on an island of five acres of grassland belonging to Mrs Tatham, with another 50 acres of arable and grassland to let nearby – enough for a small dairy herd. As the farmhouse was already occupied, Mr Candy bought a half-acre plot of land nearby to build a house, one of the first in what is now Picklers Hill. He and his wife Kitty, with their two young children, worked seven days a week to build up their dairy business. This was village life as some may remember it from their childhood.

*The field where these cows are grazing
is now Shelley Close.*

The Candy children, Michael and David, with their friend Jill Bolton, enjoy bringing in the hay in 1938.

Another family who moved to Abingdon at this time were the Harveys. In 1939, Mr Harvey was appointed head teacher of Boxhill Secondary School (now St Nicolas Primary School). The family moved to Abingdon on the day war was declared, September 3rd 1939, with their two children, Hugh and Gwyneth, soon to be joined by a new baby. Gwyneth remembered playing alongside the river Stert before the houses in Sellwood Road and South Avenue were built, in meadows full of wild flowers – kingcups, ladies' mantle and wild orchids – and at spawning time the water would be black with elvers (baby eels). Eels were still common

in the Thames at that time. Hugh had a bicycle and would explore the countryside. Early in 1940, Abingdon airfield was bombed. Not much damage was done, but Hugh found a piece of bomb casing in a crater in Northcourt, much to the admiration of his friends. Later in 1940 he was in Abingdon by the bridge where the river was packed with small boats including Salter's river steamers. They were being fuelled up at the boatyard for the journey to Dunkirk. Not all of them came back and Hugh noticed that many were damaged.

As soon as war was declared, two of James Candy's milk roundsmen were called up – one was in the middle of his milk round and Mr Candy had to step in and finish the job! He also had to find extra milk for all the evacuee children from London.

Land Army girls with James Candy (second right).

A Land Army girl milking in the Dairy Yard.

Girls from the Women's Land Army helped to keep the farm going, milking cows, haymaking and harvesting, although most of them had no experience of farming. Later in the war, Italian and German prisoners of war were delivered to the farm by lorry and Mrs Candy, whose fourth child, Jennifer, had been born in 1943, provided them with a cooked lunch every day.

Philip Candy remembers the war. One night they heard and saw what seemed to be hundreds of German bombers on their way to bomb what was later thought to be Coventry. Not long after, they heard and saw the planes returning. There was an air raid shelter available in Picklers Hill, but their mother preferred to put them under the stairs. Later, American armament carriers, tanks and heavy guns stopped for two nights in Picklers Hill fields, and his older brothers were allowed to climb on the tanks. Other American convoys threw sweets to the children. It is easy to forget that the A34 main road used to run through the centre of Abingdon.

What a relief when VE Day (Victory in Europe) was declared. The celebrations in Northcourt included a fancy dress party. The splendid photograph on page 41 belongs to Peter Maddley, who is fifth from the right in the back row. Michael Candy is the pirate at the right of the back row, and David Candy is the Cossack in the second row from the back.

The VE Day celebrations at Northcourt on 8th May 1945 included this fancy dress party. Peter Maddley is fifth from the right in the back row with Michael Candy as a pirate (end of row) and David Candy the Cossack. The girl second left in the front row is a Stopps.

9 – Post-War Development

As much of the pasture land was lost to housing in the post-war building boom, Mr Candy developed the dairy business, bringing in milk from Wantage and elsewhere.

1946 was an important year for the Candys. Realising the importance of security of tenure, Mr Candy was able to buy Northcourt Farm with its five acres of grassland. In 1947 he sold part of

Candy's Dairy in the yard of Northcourt Farm, around 1945.

Candy's Dairy milk van.

the field to a group of ex-servicemen who wanted to start a football club, now the Abingdon United Football Club, which had been formed in 1946. In 1949 a small group of people organised a cricket club playing friendly matches against other local sides. This evolved into the North Abingdon Cricket Club, which in 1953 was able to buy another part of the field, and the tithe barn was sold for conversion to a church. These three sales enabled Mr Candy to install a pasteurization plant and rotary bottle filler.

The Candy family sold land for a pitch to Abingdon United Football Club in 1947. The club has gone from strength to strength, and the same pitch is in use today.

By 1951, due to the post-war housing shortage, there were no fewer than 18 caravans parked on the farm to house local workers, with a small shop, Creasey's, on the forecourt. The Northcourt Stores and Post Office had opened in 1950. Despite many changes of ownership and name, it still thrives, currently as a Co-op. In 1958, Mr Candy opened a dairy shop in one of the old farm buildings.

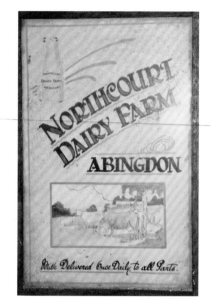

Northcourt Dairy Farm advertisement.

James Candy with two of his four children, Philip and Jenny, and their cousin Jane Candy (right) outside the new dairy shop on Northcourt Road in 1958.

Candy's Dairy expanded with the take-over of other dairies in the area to become the Argyle & Candy Dairy, and later became part of Unigate, one of the largest dairies in the country. By the 1970s the old bothy had become redundant and was being used as an apple store. Mr Candy, the ,owner tried hard to find another home for it but without success, so he regretfully demolished it when his dairy business needed space for a new office block.

Development speeded up in the post-war period

The Abingdon & Witney College of Further Education in Northcourt Road.

with South Avenue, Picklers Hill, and the Harwell estates and council housing round Appleford Drive, Hendred Way and Welford Gardens, and along Brookside and Whitelock Road. The increase in population resulted in a need for new schools, firstly Dunmore Junior and Senior Schools, and then Fitzharrys Secondary School, both on Northcourt Road, which has probably seen more changes than any other road in Abingdon.

Northcourt Road extends to the Wootton Road and is a hub for education, with the Abingdon & Witney College of Education occupying a large site on the corner of Northcourt and Wootton Road. The pressure for new housing has seen the two school caretakers' bungalows demolished and replaced with modern blocks of flats. More recently, several of the 1930s detached houses in large plots of half an acre or more have been demolished to create new housing estates, and two large houses near the entrance to Dunmore School have suffered the same fate.

Northcourt Road was the first road in the area to be given speed humps to deter speeding drivers – all of different designs as they were experimental. The south side of the road has wide grass verges planted with flowering cherry trees. St Mary's Green is still an open space surrounded by former council houses, now privately owned, and Collingwood Close, a small development of retirement bungalows.

New housing estates lie behind these modern flats and remaining 1930s houses.

10 – Church and Community

All Saints Methodist Church opened in Dorchester Crescent in 1959, and St Helen's Parish Council saw the need for an Anglican place of worship in Northcourt. This was originally going to be a new church on St Mary's Green off Northcourt Road, and the Parish appointed the Rev. Ron Hubbard as Curate for the area. He had been an architect before his ordination and thought that the Northcourt Tithe Barn, which was now redundant, would make a beautiful place of worship, as did his friend Mr Emil Godfrey, architect to the Friends of Abingdon and a specialist in the restoration of old buildings. However, not everyone was in favour of the old barn. Discouraged by the lack of local support for the project, Mr. Hubbard moved to another parish in November 1957.

There is a widely held belief that science and Christianity are incompatible, but in fact many of the scientists who came to work at Harwell and the Rutherford and Appleton Laboratories in the 1950s were committed Christians, characterised by a personal belief in Jesus, in the power of prayer, and the importance of the Bible.

During the interregnum, a group

All Saints Methodist Church.

The old Tatham Memorial Hall.

The modern Northcourt Centre
replaced the Tatham Hall in 1969.

of these local Christians was meeting for bible studies in 51 Northcourt Road (the Old House), home of Mrs Constance Cox, a former mayor of Abingdon. They prayed that God would send the right person to be Curate of Northcourt. Interviews were arranged for several candidates but they all withdrew for different reasons, leaving the Rev. John Moore – who had just completed his second curacy – as the only candidate, to the delight of the local Christians. John and his wife Mary moved into the newly-decorated vicarage on Northcourt Road in 1958 and were soon holding Sunday services in the Tatham Hall, an old army hut on the site of the present Northcourt Centre. To make the building fit for a service it was necessary

to open all the windows to clear the smoke, and to remove the debris from the previous Saturday-night social.

Meanwhile, opposition to the barn project had subsided, but negotiations to buy the barn proved unexpectedly difficult. These included how to deal with the people living in caravans on the site, what to do with the lease of Creasey's shop on the forecourt, and where to find alternative premises for the wholesale baker, whose pie trays were stored in the barn. The problems were eventually resolved and the purchase of the barn was completed in mid 1960, by which time the plans for the conversion had been completed and funding

The (dilapidated) tithe barn before conversion.

was in place, helped by existing parishioners from the town churches.

The work of conversion to a church was a herculean task, much being done by volunteer labour, including young men from the new AERE hostel on Hendred Way (now demolished for housing).

John Moore was the ideal person to be involved

The Rev. John Moore building the pulpit base.

in such a project. One of twelve children from a Welsh farming family, he was a very practical man, sourcing surplus stone from the old abbey site and the mill for the lectern and the pulpit base, which he constructed himself.

As the barn is a listed historic building, as little structural alteration as possible was made. The old waggon-doors were replaced by two large windows made, like the transept door, of Afromosia wood. The slit windows were filled with thick glass specially made by Pilkington's, using cardboard templates of each window as a guide as they are all slightly different.

The roof had to be repaired and insulated, and the walls scraped and scrubbed before new whitewash could be put on. There were moments of drama, as when John Bromley, the Clerk of Works, found the tiles slipping beneath him as he worked on the roof; and when helpers digging in the earth floor narrowly missed a pile of buried revolver shells left there by the Home Guard during the war. One night a storm threatened to lift the roof timbers, and a Saturday morning found the new Curate desperately trying to spread a rapidly-setting lorry load of ready-mixed concrete on the church floor.

Interior of Christ Church. The gloomy old barn was transformed into a joyful, light-filled space for the Service of Dedication. The original dorsal curtain of white silk decorated with crowns was painted by the assistant architect.

Drawing of Christ Church by Ken Messer showing the 1970s extension of coffee lounge and upper room.

The church project excited much local interest and generosity. The Holy Table and Communion Rails were made by local craftsmen and given by the boys of Abingdon School. The square Abingdon Cross surmounted by the Star of David (representing the Old Testament) was made by the metalwork master of Larkmead School . The splendid font stones had been unearthed some years earlier in the Dairy Yard. The cost of their cutting and erection was met by the worldwide Candy family and the silver candlesticks were presented by the Vicar of Abingdon.

Christ Church opened in the newly-restored Tithe Barn in 1961. Since then, the premises have been extended to include a hall and kitchen, a coffee lounge and upper room, an enlarged entrance hall, library and offices. The church now has one of the largest congregations in Oxfordshire.

The old milking parlour (right), now clergy offices, with the office block (left) and the Old Farmhouse behind. The former dairy yard provides valuable car parking space.

After a lifetime in Christian ministry, John and Mary Moore retired to Abingdon. Their ashes are buried outside the church which they helped to found.

In 1978 Clifford Dairies at Bracknell amalgamated with Argyle & Candy. James Candy retired in 1982, after a commitment of sixty years, but the company continued to expand under the leadership of his son Philip, taking over more companies. By 1993 it had become the sixth largest dairy company in the country with 3,000 employees. It was sold to Unigate, but the Candy family retained ownership of the Northcourt Farm site.

When Unigate finally vacated Northcourt Farm, Christ Church was able first to lease and then to buy the remaining farm buildings, greatly helped by Bill and Rosemary Buchan who moved their children's nursery business into the old milking parlour until the church was ready to purchase the site.

11 – Northcourt Today

The Northcourt land is now almost completely covered by housing estates – Dunmore Farm, Peachcroft with its shops, pub, community hall and church centre (jointly run by the Methodist and Anglican churches) and Long Furlong with a medical centre and primary school – with further expansion planned for the area between Dunmore Road and Lodge Hill.

Abingdon's character of a country town surrounded by farms is long gone. At one time there were nine farms around the town; now the only remaining farm is Peachcroft, and in order to survive it has diversified with a pick-your-own business, turkeys and geese for Christmas, a farm shop and cafe, and car boot sales in the summer months. The fine old barn here has been modernised to provide a venue for meetings and exhibitions such as Abingdon Artists' summer show.

Northcourt now has a small supermarket with a post office; the newsagents closed in 2021 and now hosts a take-away pizza outlet. With three

Map of Northcourt today.

Dunmore School 'lollipop lady', Mrs Beryl Horne. Mrs Horne later crossed children outside John Mason School.

primary schools – Dunmore, Rush Common and Long Furlong – Fitzharrys Secondary School and a College of Education, the area is very popular with families of school-age children.

The old Tatham Hall was replaced in 1968 by the present Northcourt Centre, which opened in 1969.

It provides good facilities for many groups, from ballet and Scottish Country Dancing, two local Women's Institutes and the Abingdon Archaeology & History Society, to the Spring and Autumn Shows of the Abingdon Horticultural Society.

The Boundary House is a very popular eatery,

especially in the summer with its large garden. The Spread Eagle pub on Northcourt Road has expanded into the neighbouring property and is now a flourishing restaurant.

The old barns along Northcourt Road have been sensitively converted, with a cafe and drop-in centre in the smaller barn and a splendid function room in the large barn, and the Church's dream of creating a focal point for the whole Northcourt community has become a reality.

Northcourt has always been closely connected with Abingdon, but it has also always had its own distinctive character. Even though the hamlet has been completely absorbed into the suburbs of Abingdon and nearly all the farmland has been built over, with its old barns, cottages, and remaining green fields, Northcourt Farm is still at the heart of the local community, as it has been throughout its history.

This book has tried to capture some of the long history which has shaped the Northcourt of today.

Northcourt barns, now converted for church and community use.

Sources

Northcourt Enclosure Map and Award, of 1841

St Helen's Parish Tithe Map and Award, 1842

Census, 1881

J. Townsend, *A History of Abingdon* (1910)

A.E. Preston, *St. Nicholas Abingdon and other papers* (1927)

Abingdon Corporation, *Road to the Seventies* (1970)

M. Gosling, *Northcourt: Portrait of Hamlet* (unpublished Local History Thesis, 1983)

James S. Candy, *A Tapestry of Life* (1984)

Christ Church, the Making of a Church (1986)

M. Cox, *The Story of Abingdon* (4 volumes) (1986)

N. Hood, *William Teulon Blandford Fletcher 1858-1936* (1986)

C.F. Slade & and G. Lambrick, *Two Cartularies of Abingdon Abbey* (1990)

J. Thomas & E. Drury, *More of Abingdon Past & Present* (2008)